"Beyond the Brush: AI's Revolution in Art and Film"

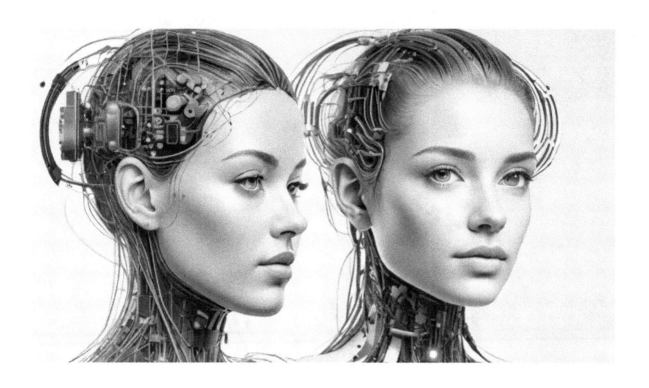

Introduction:

Chapter 1: The Magic Behind Generative AI

1.1 What is Generative AI?

Generative AI refers to artificial intelligence that creates new content or data based on patterns it has learned from existing data. It's like teaching a machine to be creative by showing it a lot of examples. Imagine having a super-smart assistant that can paint, write, or design just like a human artist.

Example: Think of it as a digital artist who has seen thousands of paintings and can now create a new piece that looks like it belongs in a gallery, even though it never existed before.

1.2 How Does It Work?

At its core, generative AI uses algorithms called neural networks. These networks are inspired by the human brain and are designed to recognize patterns and generate new content.

- **Training Data:** The AI learns from vast amounts of existing data. For example, if you want it to generate new art, you feed it thousands of paintings.
- **Patterns and Algorithms:** The AI uses complex mathematical formulas to understand the patterns in the data and then creates something new based on those patterns.

Interactive Example: Imagine a recipe book where you learn to cook by practicing many dishes. Generative AI is like that recipe book, but instead of food, it's learning to create art, music, or visuals.

Chapter 2: Generative AI for Artists

2.1 Creating New Artwork

Generative AI can assist artists by creating initial drafts, exploring different styles, or even generating entire artworks.

Example: An artist can use AI tools like DALL-E or Midjourney to generate a concept for a painting based on a description like "a serene landscape at sunrise." The AI can produce several options, helping the artist choose or get inspired.

2.2 Enhancing Creativity

AI can suggest new color palettes, compositions, or styles, allowing artists to experiment beyond their usual techniques.

Example: If you're an illustrator working on a fantasy scene, the AI might suggest adding elements like mythical creatures or alternative color schemes to enrich the scene.

2.3 Speeding Up the Process

Generative AI can automate repetitive tasks like filling in backgrounds or generating texture patterns, freeing artists to focus on more complex and creative aspects of their work.

Example: An artist might use AI to quickly generate a series of background textures for a digital painting, saving hours of manual work.

Chapter 3: Generative AI in Filmmaking

3.1 Scriptwriting Assistance

Generative AI can help screenwriters by suggesting plot twists, dialogue, or character development ideas based on a given theme or genre.

Example: A writer could use AI to brainstorm different endings for a film script, helping to refine the story and explore various creative directions.

3.2 Visual Storyboarding

AI tools can generate storyboards from script descriptions, helping filmmakers visualize scenes before actual production begins.

Example: By inputting a scene description into an AI tool, filmmakers can get a series of storyboard frames that represent the action, helping to plan shots and camera angles.

3.3 Post-Production and Editing

AI can assist in editing by automating tasks like color correction, audio syncing, and even creating visual effects.

Example: During editing, AI tools can automatically adjust the lighting and color grading of each scene, ensuring consistency throughout the film.

Chapter 4: Generative AI in CGI and VFX

4.1 Creating Realistic 3D Models

Generative AI can help design realistic 3D models for characters, objects, and environments based on provided specifications.

Example: For a sci-fi movie, AI can generate detailed 3D models of futuristic gadgets or alien creatures, speeding up the design process.

4.2 Enhancing Visual Effects

AI can be used to create or enhance visual effects by simulating realistic environmental effects like smoke, fire, or water.

Example: In a fantasy film, AI can generate realistic dragon fire or magical effects that blend seamlessly with live-action footage.

4.3 Automating Animation

AI tools can automate certain aspects of animation, such as generating in-between frames or creating realistic movements based on motion capture data.

Example: An AI system can take a few keyframes of an animated character and generate the in-between frames needed for smooth motion, saving animators a lot of time.

Chapter 5: Getting Started with Generative AI

5.1 Choosing the Right Tools

There are various AI tools available for different artistic needs. Here's how to pick the right one:

- **For Art:** Tools like DALL-E or Midjourney for creating images from text prompts.

- **For Filmmaking:** Tools like ScriptAI for scriptwriting or DeepArt for visual effects.

- **For CGI/VFX:** Tools like Blender with AI plugins for 3D modeling and animation.

5.2 Learning and Integration

Start by experimenting with free or trial versions of these tools. Many come with tutorials to help you learn.

Interactive Example: Follow a step-by-step tutorial where you use an AI tool to generate a piece of art or create a storyboard for a short film. Document your process and reflect on the results.

5.3 Ethical Considerations

Be mindful of the ethical implications of using AI, such as ensuring that generated content respects copyright and is used responsibly.

Example: Always verify that the AI-generated content is original and doesn't infringe on the rights of other creators.

Chapter 6: Case Studies and Success Stories

6.1 Artistic Triumphs

Explore real-world examples of artists who have successfully integrated AI into their work.

Example: An artist used AI to create a series of digital paintings that were showcased in a major art gallery, illustrating how AI can enhance artistic expression.

6.2 Filmmaking Innovations

Look at how filmmakers have utilized AI to streamline their processes and achieve groundbreaking results.

Example: A filmmaker used AI for visual effects in a blockbuster film, leading to innovative scenes that captivated audiences.

6.3 CGI and VFX Milestones

Learn about notable projects in CGI and VFX where AI played a crucial role in achieving high-quality results.

Example: A VFX studio used AI to generate complex animations for a major video game, demonstrating AI's potential in the gaming industry.

Chapter 7: Future Trends and Innovations

7.1 The Evolution of Generative AI

Discuss how generative AI is expected to evolve and its potential future applications in art, filmmaking, and VFX.

7.2 Embracing the Future

Encourage readers to stay updated with the latest advancements and continue experimenting with AI to push the boundaries of creativity.

Interactive Example: Set up a small project where readers use a new AI tool to create something unique, encouraging them to share their results and experiences.

Conclusion

Generative AI is transforming the creative landscape by offering new tools and opportunities for artists, filmmakers, and VFX professionals. By understanding and leveraging these technologies, creatives can enhance their work, streamline processes, and explore new realms of artistic expression.

This guide aims to be both informative and engaging, providing a clear path from understanding generative AI to applying it in various creative fields.

Chapter 1:

The Magic Behind

Generative AI

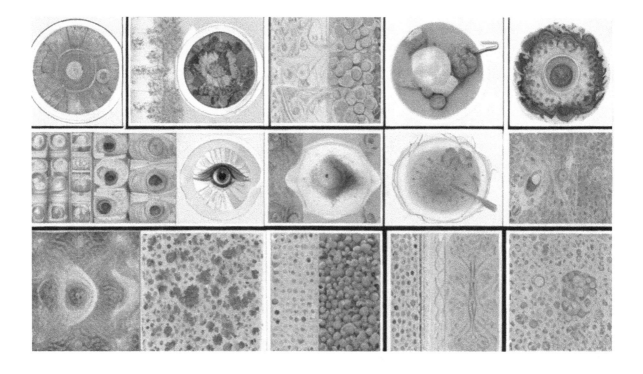

Scene:

In a cozy attic room bathed in the warm glow of vintage lamps, Emma, a young artist with a passion for discovery, finds herself amidst an array of ancient books, curious artifacts, and intriguing gadgets. The air is thick with the scent of old parchment and the promise of hidden secrets. Across from her sits Alex, an enigmatic figure whose deep understanding of technology is matched only by his sense of wonder.

The golden light casts playful shadows across the walls, where AI-generated artworks hang like modern-day masterpieces waiting to be explored.

Emma: (holding up a dusty, ornate book with "Generative AI: The Art of Machine Creativity" embossed in gold) "Alex, I found this old tome up here. It's labeled 'Generative AI: The Art of Machine Creativity.' What exactly is Generative AI?"

Alex: (his eyes twinkling with enthusiasm) "Ah, Generative AI! Imagine it as a magical assistant with boundless imagination. It's like having a creative partner who never sleeps and can conjure up new ideas from the ether of digital creativity. Let me paint a picture for you."

Emma: (raising an eyebrow) "Paint a picture? You mean like with paint and brushes?"

Alex: (chuckling) "In a manner of speaking, yes! Imagine a super-smart assistant that's seen thousands of paintings, read countless stories, and designed myriad objects. This assistant can then create something entirely new—something that feels like it belongs in a gallery or on a best-seller list, even though it's never existed before."

Emma: (leaning in with interest) "So, this assistant is creating things on its own? How does it manage that?"

Alex: "Exactly! Generative AI is designed to be creative by learning from existing data. It doesn't just mimic; it generates new content by analyzing patterns and characteristics from what it has learned. It's a bit like having an artist who's absorbed every style and technique but creates something fresh and unique."

Emma: (eyes wide) "That sounds incredible! How does it learn to be so creative? What's the process?"

Alex: "Great question. The magic happens through something called neural networks. These are sophisticated algorithms inspired by the way the human brain works. They help the AI recognize patterns and relationships within data."

Emma: "Neural networks? That sounds complex. How do they work?"

Alex: "Imagine your brain as you're learning to paint. You observe different styles, techniques, and colors. Over time, you start to recognize patterns and can apply them to your own work. Neural networks work in a similar way. They process information through layers of nodes, each layer extracting different features from the data."

Emma: (nodding) "So, the AI looks at a lot of examples and learns from them?"

Alex: "Exactly. Think of it like feeding the AI a rich diet of diverse artistic styles and content. The more it learns, the better it becomes at understanding and recreating those styles in new ways."

Emma: "And how does the AI come up with something new from all this learned information?"

Alex: "The AI uses complex mathematical formulas to mix and match the patterns it has learned. It's akin to combining ingredients in a recipe. By blending different elements it has studied, it creates something novel yet familiar."

Emma: "That sounds fascinating! How does the AI know what to create?"

Alex: "You, as the user, provide prompts or descriptions. For instance, if you ask it to generate an image of a 'serene landscape at sunrise,' it uses its understanding of landscapes, colors, and lighting to create a new image based on your description."

Emma: (excitedly) "So, if I wanted to see a painting of a fantastical cityscape, the AI could create that too?"

Alex: "Absolutely! The AI can generate a vast range of images, stories, or designs based on the parameters you provide. It's like having an endless canvas where your imagination is the only limit."

Emma: "That's amazing! Can it also create music or write stories?"

Alex: "Yes, indeed. Generative AI isn't limited to visual art. It can compose music, generate melodies and harmonies, and write stories, poems, or scripts based on the styles and genres you specify."

Emma: "I'm so impressed. It seems like AI could really transform how we create art and tell stories."

Alex: "Indeed, it has the potential to revolutionize creative fields. With Generative AI, artists and creators have a powerful tool that allows them to explore new ideas and push the boundaries of traditional art forms."

Emma: "But how does the AI ensure that the creativity it produces feels authentic?"

Alex: "That's a key point. While AI doesn't have emotions or personal experiences like humans, it mimics creativity by generating content based on diverse inputs. The authenticity comes from how you, as the creator, use these tools to infuse personal meaning and direction into the AI-generated content."

Emma: "So, the AI provides the raw materials, and I use my vision and creativity to shape it?"

Alex: "Exactly. The AI acts as a collaborator, offering fresh perspectives and possibilities. It's up to you to guide and refine these outputs to align with your artistic vision."

Emma: "I can see how this could be a game-changer for artists. It opens up so many new avenues for creativity."

Alex: "Absolutely. The magic of Generative AI lies in its ability to enhance and expand human creativity, making it easier to explore new ideas and create works that might not have been possible otherwise."

Emma: (thoughtfully) "I'm excited to dive into this. It feels like opening a door to a whole new realm of artistic expression."

Alex: "And that's the essence of it. Generative AI is like a key that unlocks new creative dimensions. It's a tool that can help you discover uncharted territories in your art, filmmaking, or any other creative endeavor."

Emma: "I'm eager to start experimenting. Can you show me how to use some of these tools?"

Alex: (nodding with a smile) "Of course. We'll begin with a basic introduction to the tools and how to interact with them. It's a fascinating journey ahead, and I'm thrilled to guide you through it."

Emma: "Thank you, Alex. I feel like I've just scratched the surface of something truly extraordinary."

Alex: "You have, Emma. And remember, this is just the beginning. With Generative AI, the possibilities are as boundless as your imagination."

Scene:

As Emma and Alex delve deeper into the world of Generative AI, the room around them seems to shimmer with the possibilities of creativity. The dusty tome opens to reveal a wealth of knowledge, setting the stage for a new chapter in Emma's artistic journey. The golden light dances across the walls, reflecting the infinite potential that lies ahead in their exploration of machine creativity.

This dialogue-driven chapter aims to engage readers with a blend of curiosity and wonder, making the complex concepts of Generative AI accessible and intriguing. The narrative style provides a rich, immersive experience that both informs and entertains.

Chapter 1.2: How Does It Work?

Scene:

The attic room is now dimly lit, with soft shadows flickering across the walls as Alex and Emma settle into comfortable armchairs. The golden light from the lamps creates a warm, inviting atmosphere, perfect for diving into the intricacies of Generative AI. Alex has brought out a chalkboard with colorful diagrams, ready to illustrate the core concepts.

Emma: (looking at the chalkboard) "Alright, Alex, you've piqued my curiosity. I understand that Generative AI can create amazing new things, but how does it actually work? What's happening behind the scenes?"

Alex: (smiling and drawing a neural network diagram) "Great question, Emma. At the heart of Generative AI are algorithms called neural networks. Think of them as complex systems inspired by the human brain. Let me break it down for you."

Emma: (leaning closer) "I'm all ears. How do these neural networks work?"

Alex: "Imagine the human brain as a massive network of neurons. Each neuron connects with many others, passing along information. Neural networks in AI work similarly, with layers of interconnected nodes or 'neurons.' These networks process data through these connections to recognize patterns and make decisions."

Emma: "So, it's like a digital version of our brain?"

Alex: "Exactly! But instead of biological neurons, we have artificial ones. These networks analyze data, find patterns, and learn from them. Now, let's dive into how this process unfolds."

Emma: "I'm ready. What's the first step?"

Alex: "The first step is called 'training.' This is where the AI learns from vast amounts of existing data. For instance, if we want an AI to generate new artwork, we feed it thousands of paintings. This collection of artworks becomes the 'training data.'"

Emma: "So, it's like showing the AI a huge gallery of paintings?"

Alex: "Exactly! The AI looks at these paintings to understand various styles, colors, techniques, and compositions. It's like feeding it a buffet of artistic knowledge. The more diverse and extensive the data, the richer the AI's learning experience."

Emma: "Got it. And what happens after the AI has seen all this data?"

Alex: "Next, the AI uses complex mathematical formulas, called algorithms, to analyze and interpret the patterns in the data. These algorithms help the AI understand how different elements in the artwork relate to each other."

Emma: "Can you give me an example of how this works?"

Alex: "Sure! Imagine you're learning to cook by following recipes. At first, you follow the instructions exactly, but over time, you start to recognize patterns in the recipes—how different ingredients combine to create flavors. You then use this understanding to experiment and create your own dishes."

Emma: "Ah, so the AI is like a chef learning from recipes!"

Alex: "Precisely! The AI learns from the 'recipes' of the artworks—the colors, brush strokes, composition, and so on. It then uses this knowledge to generate new pieces. For instance, if you ask the AI to create a painting of a 'sunset over a mountain range,' it uses its understanding of sunsets, mountains, and painting styles to create a new, unique image."

Emma: "That's fascinating! So, the AI is combining what it has learned to make something new?"

Alex: "Exactly. The AI uses its understanding of the patterns and relationships in the data to generate new content. It's like combining ingredients from different recipes to create a new dish. The result is something that feels both fresh and familiar."

Emma: "I see! And how does the AI ensure that the new creations are original?"

Alex: "Great question. While the AI generates content based on what it has learned, it doesn't simply copy existing works. Instead, it mixes and matches patterns in creative ways. The result is a synthesis of the learned patterns rather than a direct replication of any one piece."

Emma: "That sounds like a very sophisticated process. Is there any interaction involved in this generation process?"

Alex: "Yes, there is! As the user, you provide prompts or descriptions that guide the AI. For example, if you want a piece of art depicting 'a futuristic cityscape,' the AI takes this input and uses its learned patterns to generate an image that matches the description."

Emma: (thoughtfully) "So, the AI is like a creative partner that takes my ideas and turns them into something tangible?"

Alex: "Exactly. You provide the vision, and the AI helps bring it to life by applying its learned knowledge in new and innovative ways."

Emma: "That's incredible. Can you show me how this works with a practical example?"

Alex: (nodding) "Absolutely. Let's start with a simple example. Imagine we want to generate an image of a 'whimsical forest with glowing mushrooms.' I'll input this description into the AI, and we'll see how it combines its understanding of forests, mushrooms, and whimsical elements to create something unique."

Emma: (excitedly) "I can't wait to see it!"

Alex: (typing on a laptop and showing Emma the AI-generated image) "Here we go. This is what the AI came up with based on our description."

Emma: (amazed) "Wow, that's beautiful! It's like the AI took the essence of what we described and turned it into something magical."

Alex: "Exactly. The AI's ability to blend learned patterns with user inputs creates truly unique results. It's a collaboration between your creativity and the AI's vast knowledge."

Emma: "I'm so excited to explore this further. It feels like opening a treasure chest of possibilities!"

Alex: "And that's the essence of Generative AI. It's a tool that enhances and expands human creativity, offering endless opportunities for exploration and innovation."

Scene:

As Alex and Emma continue to explore the capabilities of Generative AI, the room seems to buzz with the energy of creative potential. The chalkboard, filled with diagrams and explanations, now serves as a gateway to a world where imagination and technology converge in extraordinary ways. The warmth of the golden light reflects the excitement of their discovery, setting the stage for new creative adventures.

This detailed and immersive dialogue provides a comprehensive yet accessible explanation of how Generative AI works, using relatable analogies and interactive examples to engage readers and demystify the technology.

Chapter 2: Generative AI for Artists

2.1 Creating New Artwork

Scene:

In a sunlit studio cluttered with paintbrushes, canvases, and sketchbooks, Maya, an established painter, is having a conversation with Sam, a digital art enthusiast who's been experimenting with Generative AI tools. The walls are adorned with Maya's vibrant artworks, and a sleek computer sits at the center of the room, ready for their exploration.

Maya: (brushing strokes of color onto a canvas) "Sam, I've heard a lot about Generative AI lately. How exactly can it help me with my artwork?"

Sam: (setting up the computer) "Great question, Maya! Generative AI can be a fantastic tool for artists. It can help with creating initial drafts, exploring new styles, or even generating entire artworks from scratch. Let me show you how it works."

Maya: (intrigued) "That sounds interesting. How does it start?"

Sam: "Let's dive into a practical example. Imagine you want to create a painting of a serene landscape at sunrise. With Generative AI tools like DALL-E or Midjourney, you can start by providing a description, and the AI generates several options based on that description."

Maya: (nodding) "Okay, so it's like giving the AI a theme or idea to work with?"

Sam: "Exactly! You give it a prompt, like 'a serene landscape at sunrise,' and it uses its trained knowledge to create different visual interpretations of that scene. Let's try it out."

Maya: (watching as Sam types on the computer) "What are you doing now?"

Sam: "I'm inputting our description into the AI tool. It's processing the prompt and generating images based on the patterns it has learned from various landscapes and sunrise paintings."

Maya: (excitedly) "I'm curious to see the results."

Sam: (after a few moments) "Here are the options the AI generated. Take a look."

Maya: (examining the screen) "Wow, these are stunning! Each one has a unique interpretation of a sunrise landscape. It's like having multiple drafts to choose from."

Sam: "Exactly. You can use these AI-generated images as initial drafts or inspiration. It's a way to quickly explore different visual ideas without starting from scratch."

Maya: (thoughtfully) "I see the potential here. It could really help me brainstorm and refine my ideas before committing to a final piece."

Sam: "Absolutely. And it's not just about generating drafts. The AI can also help you explore different styles. For instance, you could ask it to create a sunrise landscape in the style of impressionism, cubism, or any other art movement."

Maya: (intrigued) "That sounds fascinating. How would that work?"

Sam: "You simply provide the style you're interested in, along with your subject description. The AI then combines its knowledge of that style with your subject to create something unique."

Maya: (excitedly) "Let's give it a try! I'd love to see a sunrise landscape in the style of Van Gogh."

Sam: (typing on the computer) "Let's see what the AI comes up with."

Maya: (after a few moments) "These are incredible! The brush strokes and color palettes really evoke Van Gogh's style."

Sam: "Exactly. The AI has used its understanding of Van Gogh's techniques to interpret your description. This can be a great way to experiment with different styles and see how they affect your subject matter."

Maya: (thoughtfully) "I'm really impressed. It's like having an art assistant who can explore different styles and ideas with me."

Sam: "That's a perfect way to describe it. The AI is a collaborator that helps you explore possibilities and discover new creative directions."

Maya: "Can it also help with other aspects of the artistic process, like color palettes or compositions?"

Sam: "Yes, indeed. For instance, you can use AI to generate different color palettes based on a theme or emotion. You can also experiment with various compositions to see how they affect the overall feel of your artwork."

Maya: "Can we try generating a color palette for one of these images?"

Sam: (typing on the computer) "Sure, let's choose one of the sunrise landscapes and see what color palettes the AI suggests."

Maya: (watching the screen) "This is fantastic! The AI has provided several palettes that complement the mood of the painting."

Sam: "Exactly. The AI can analyze the generated images and suggest palettes that enhance the visual impact. It's like having a color theory expert right at your fingertips."

Maya: "This is amazing. I can see how AI can streamline my workflow and provide new creative avenues. It's like having a muse that never tires."

Sam: "That's a great way to put it. Generative AI is all about expanding your creative toolkit and offering new perspectives. It's not meant to replace your artistic vision but to enhance it."

Maya: (smiling) "I'm excited to incorporate these tools into my process. It feels like I've opened a door to a new world of artistic possibilities."

Sam: "I'm glad to hear that, Maya. The key is to experiment and see how these tools fit into your workflow. The AI can be a powerful ally in your creative journey."

Scene:

As Maya and Sam continue exploring the capabilities of Generative AI, the studio is filled with an air of excitement and possibility. The computer screen showcases a variety of AI-generated artworks, color palettes, and compositions, each reflecting a new facet of artistic exploration. The warm sunlight streaming through the window seems to mirror the creative energy that the AI tools have sparked in Maya's artistic process.

This dialogue-based chapter introduces artists to how Generative AI can assist in creating new artwork, exploring styles, and refining ideas. It emphasizes the collaborative nature of AI tools, making the technology accessible and inspiring for artists seeking to expand their creative horizons.

2.2 Enhancing Creativity

Scene:

In a vibrant artist's studio, filled with eclectic pieces of artwork and art supplies, Elena, a fantasy illustrator, is chatting with Jordan, a seasoned digital artist and AI enthusiast. The space is lively, with the walls decorated by Elena's fantastical illustrations of mythical landscapes and creatures. An array of colorful palettes and sketches are strewn across the table, and a computer stands ready for their creative exploration.

Elena: (studying a sketch of a mystical forest) "Jordan, I'm working on this fantasy scene, but I feel like it's missing something. I want to bring more magic and depth to it. Can AI help with that?"

Jordan: (sitting down at the computer) "Absolutely, Elena! AI can be a fantastic tool for enhancing your creativity. It can suggest new color palettes, compositions, and even elements to add to your scene. Let's see how it can enrich your mystical forest."

Elena: (curious) "That sounds promising. How do we start?"

Jordan: "Let's begin by exploring some alternative color palettes. You can input a description of the mood or atmosphere you want to create, and the AI can suggest colors that fit that vision."

Elena: (typing on the computer) "I'm thinking of a magical twilight setting with deep blues and purples. Let's see what the AI comes up with."

Jordan: (clicking a few buttons) "The AI will generate color palettes that evoke the mystical and magical feel you're aiming for."

Elena: (watching the screen) "Wow, these palettes are gorgeous! They range from soft, ethereal blues to rich, mysterious purples. Each one creates a different mood."

Jordan: "Exactly. The AI can provide a range of palettes to suit various aspects of your scene. It's like having a color consultant who understands the mood and atmosphere you want to convey."

Elena: (enthusiastically) "I can see how these palettes could dramatically change the look of my scene. What about composition? Can AI assist with that as well?"

Jordan: "Definitely. AI can help by suggesting different compositions based on the elements in your scene. It can offer layouts that enhance visual interest and balance."

Elena: "Great! I'd love to explore some composition options. How do we proceed?"

Jordan: (loading an AI composition tool) "We'll input the key elements of your scene, like the mystical forest, any mythical creatures, and other major features. The AI will then suggest various ways to arrange these elements for optimal visual impact."

Elena: (typing in the details) "I've included the forest, a magical stream, and a few ancient trees. Let's see what the AI suggests."

Jordan: (clicking the generate button) "Let's check out the AI's composition suggestions."

Elena: (examining the results) "These compositions are fascinating! Some emphasize the stream as the focal point, while others create a sense of depth by arranging the trees and magical elements differently."

Jordan: "The AI uses patterns from countless artworks to suggest compositions that can enhance the overall visual appeal. It's like having a team of design experts offering you new perspectives."

Elena: "This is fantastic! Now, can AI help with adding elements to the scene? I feel like the forest could use some additional magical touches."

Jordan: "Absolutely. You can describe the type of elements you're considering, and the AI can suggest additions that fit seamlessly into your scene."

Elena: "I'd like to add some mythical creatures and perhaps some glowing plants. Can the AI provide suggestions for that?"

Jordan: (typing on the computer) "Let's input those details and see what the AI suggests."

Elena: (after a moment) "These suggestions are amazing! The AI proposed various mythical creatures like fairy-like beings and glowing, bioluminescent plants. They all fit perfectly with the magical atmosphere."

Jordan: "That's the beauty of it. The AI can generate ideas that you might not have considered, adding new dimensions to your artwork."

Elena: "This feels like having an endless source of inspiration. The AI is helping me push beyond my usual techniques and explore new creative avenues."

Jordan: "Exactly. The AI serves as a creative partner that can broaden your horizons and inspire fresh ideas. It's not about replacing your creativity but enhancing it."

Elena: (thoughtfully) "I'm excited to integrate these new elements and compositions into my artwork. It's like unlocking a new level of creativity."

Jordan: "I'm glad you're finding it useful. Remember, the AI is here to complement your vision and help you explore new possibilities. Keep experimenting and see where it takes you."

Elena: "Thank you, Jordan. This has been incredibly inspiring. I feel like I have a whole new set of tools to play with."

Jordan: "You're welcome, Elena. The world of Generative AI is vast and full of potential. Enjoy the journey of discovery and creativity!"

Scene:

As Elena and Jordan wrap up their session, the studio is filled with a sense of accomplishment and excitement. The computer screen displays a vibrant array of new color palettes, compositions, and magical elements, each contributing to the rich tapestry of Elena's fantasy scene. The creative energy in the room reflects the possibilities that Generative AI has unlocked, inspiring Elena to take her art in new and exhilarating directions.

This chapter illustrates how Generative AI can enhance artistic creativity by suggesting color palettes, compositions, and additional elements. Through the dialogue, readers can see practical examples of how AI tools can be integrated into the creative process, making it accessible and exciting for artists.

2.3 Speeding Up the Process

Scene:

In a bustling art studio, filled with canvases, paints, and sketches, Jessica, a digital artist known for her intricate and detailed work, is hard at work on a large digital painting. The piece features a fantastical cityscape with towering spires and sprawling landscapes. Despite her enthusiasm, she's feeling overwhelmed by the sheer volume of repetitive tasks required to complete the painting. Enter Sam, an experienced digital art technician with a knack for AI tools.

Jessica: (sighing as she looks at her screen) "Sam, I'm swamped. This digital painting is turning out great, but the repetitive tasks, like filling in the background textures and creating patterns, are taking forever. I wish there was a way to speed this up."

Sam: (smiling knowingly) "I think I can help with that. Have you tried using Generative AI for automating some of these repetitive tasks?"

Jessica: (looking curious) "Generative AI? I've heard of it, but I didn't realize it could help with things like texture patterns. How does that work?"

Sam: "Generative AI can be a real game-changer for speeding up repetitive tasks. For example, it can quickly generate background textures, patterns, and even complex details based on your specifications. Let me show you how."

Jessica: "That sounds promising. Let's give it a try. What do we need to do?"

Sam: (sitting down at the computer) "First, we'll use an AI tool designed for generating textures and patterns. You'll provide it with some parameters, and the AI will produce a series of textures that you can use in your painting."

Jessica: (watching intently) "So, I just need to describe what kind of textures I want?"

Sam: "Exactly. Let's start by defining the type of texture you need. For your cityscape, we might want to create textures for brickwork, stone, or even magical glowing patterns."

Jessica: (typing on the computer) "I'd like textures that resemble ancient stone and some with a mystical, glowing effect. Let's see what the AI can do."

Sam: (clicking a few buttons) "Great. The AI will generate a range of textures based on your description. It uses patterns from existing textures and combines them in creative ways to produce new designs."

Jessica: (observing the screen) "This is impressive! The AI is generating textures that look like they could belong in an ancient city or a magical realm. It's so much faster than creating these from scratch."

Sam: "That's the beauty of it. The AI handles the repetitive work, allowing you to focus on the more intricate and creative aspects of your painting. You can save hours of manual work and still achieve high-quality results."

Jessica: "I can see how this would be a huge time-saver. What about other elements, like pattern designs for the city's structures?"

Sam: "AI can handle those too. You can input parameters for different patterns, such as geometric designs or intricate motifs. The AI will generate these patterns quickly and efficiently."

Jessica: "That sounds fantastic! Let's try generating some patterns for the city's spires and facades."

Sam: (inputting parameters for various patterns) "We'll use the AI to create a selection of patterns that you can choose from. You might find some that fit perfectly with your vision for the cityscape."

Jessica: (as the patterns appear) "These patterns are amazing! They range from elaborate designs to simpler, more subtle ones. It's like having a whole library of patterns at my fingertips."

Sam: "Exactly. The AI gives you a wealth of options to choose from, making it easy to find the perfect fit for your artwork. You can mix and match different elements to create a cohesive and visually stunning piece."

Jessica: "This is incredible. It's not just about saving time; it's about enhancing my creative process and exploring new possibilities."

Sam: "That's the key. Generative AI isn't just a tool for speeding up work; it's a way to expand your creative toolkit. By automating repetitive tasks, you free up more time to focus on the aspects of your art that truly inspire you."

Jessica: "I'm excited to see how these AI-generated textures and patterns will transform my cityscape. It's like I've unlocked a new level of efficiency and creativity."

Sam: "I'm glad you're finding it useful. Remember, the goal is to let AI handle the tedious tasks so you can channel your energy into the parts of your art that make it unique and personal."

Jessica: "Thank you, Sam. This has been a game-changer for me. I can't wait to integrate these elements into my painting."

Sam: "You're welcome, Jessica. Enjoy the process, and don't hesitate to explore other ways AI can assist in your creative journey. There's always something new to discover."

Scene:

As Jessica continues her work, the studio is filled with a renewed sense of excitement and creativity. The AI-generated textures and patterns seamlessly integrate into her cityscape painting, adding depth and detail that elevate the artwork. The time saved on repetitive tasks allows Jessica to focus on refining and enhancing her vision, making the creative process more enjoyable and rewarding.

This chapter demonstrates how Generative AI can streamline repetitive tasks in the artistic process. Through the dialogue, readers gain practical insights into how AI tools can be used to generate textures and patterns, ultimately saving time and enhancing creativity. The interaction between Jessica and Sam highlights the benefits of integrating AI into the workflow, making it accessible and engaging for artists.

Chapter 3: Generative AI in Filmmaking

3.1 Scriptwriting Assistance

Scene:

In a modern, sunlit office lined with shelves of screenplays and film memorabilia, Maya, a dedicated screenwriter with a passion for storytelling, sits hunched over her desk, surrounded by notes and coffee cups. Her laptop screen displays a partially written script with several lines of dialogue and a complex plot. Enter

David, a seasoned script consultant with a knack for integrating technology into the creative process.

Maya: (rubbing her temples) "David, I'm struggling with the ending of this screenplay. I've got a good setup, but I can't seem to find the right twist to make it really impactful. I've tried a few ideas, but nothing feels quite right."

David: (sitting down next to her) "I hear you. Sometimes it's hard to see the forest for the trees when you're deep into a script. Have you considered using Generative AI for brainstorming plot twists or dialogue?"

Maya: (looking curious) "Generative AI? I've heard about it in the context of art and design, but I didn't realize it could be useful for scriptwriting. How does that work?"

David: "Generative AI can be a valuable tool for scriptwriters. It can analyze existing scripts and story structures, and then generate new ideas based on the themes and genres you're working with. Let me show you how it can help."

Maya: "That sounds intriguing. How do we get started?"

David: (opening a laptop) "First, we'll use an AI scriptwriting tool. These tools are designed to assist with brainstorming and refining ideas. You'll input details about your story, such as the genre, main characters, and current plot points, and the AI will generate suggestions."

Maya: "So, we can use it to come up with different endings or even develop new dialogue?"

David: "Exactly. The AI can provide a variety of plot twists, character developments, and dialogue options. It's like having a brainstorming partner who's always ready to help. Let's start by inputting some details about your current script."

Maya: (typing on the laptop) "Okay, I've entered the main plot points and the genre of the screenplay, which is a thriller. Let's see what the AI comes up with for the ending."

David: (clicking a few buttons) "The AI will analyze the information you've provided and generate several possible endings based on similar thriller scripts and common plot structures."

Maya: (watching the screen) "Wow, look at these options! Some of these endings are totally unexpected. This one suggests a twist where the protagonist is actually working with the antagonist, and another one introduces a hidden betrayal by a trusted ally."

David: "Exactly. The AI can offer fresh perspectives and ideas that might not have occurred to you. It's great for pushing the boundaries of your story and exploring different creative directions."

Maya: "These suggestions are fantastic! I never would have thought of some of these twists on my own. How does the AI come up with these ideas?"

David: "The AI uses a combination of algorithms and pattern recognition to generate suggestions. It analyzes plot structures, character arcs, and narrative techniques from a wide range of existing scripts. By understanding these patterns, it can create new, original ideas that fit within the framework of your story."

Maya: "That's impressive. Can it also help with dialogue or character development?"

David: "Yes, it can. For dialogue, you can provide the AI with character descriptions and the context of a scene, and it will generate dialogue that fits the tone and style of your script. For character development, it can suggest backstories, motivations, and relationships based on the traits you've outlined."

Maya: "That would be incredibly useful. Let's try generating some dialogue for a crucial scene where the protagonist confronts the antagonist."

David: (inputting details into the AI tool) "I'll set the parameters for a tense confrontation between the protagonist and antagonist. The AI will generate dialogue options that fit the scene's intensity and emotional stakes."

Maya: (reading the suggestions) "These dialogues are spot on! They capture the tension and conflict perfectly. It's like the characters are coming to life in a new way."

David: "That's the power of Generative AI. It can provide dialogue that enhances character dynamics and drives the story forward. It's a great way to overcome writer's block and find new ways to express your characters' voices."

Maya: "This is incredible. I can already see how these suggestions will help refine my script and elevate it to the next level."

David: "I'm glad you're finding it helpful. Remember, the AI is a tool to assist and inspire. It's up to you to select the ideas that resonate with your vision and integrate them into your script."

Maya: "Thank you, David. This has been a game-changer for me. I'm excited to see how these new ideas will shape the final draft."

David: "You're welcome, Maya. Keep experimenting with the AI tools and let them enhance your creative process. The possibilities are endless."

Scene:

As Maya continues to work on her screenplay, the AI-generated suggestions transform her script into a more dynamic and engaging story. The plot twists and dialogue enhance the narrative, making the ending more impactful and the characters more compelling. With the help of Generative AI, Maya finds herself invigorated and inspired, ready to bring her screenplay to life with renewed enthusiasm.

This chapter demonstrates how Generative AI can be a valuable asset in scriptwriting, offering practical tools for brainstorming plot twists, developing dialogue, and refining character arcs. Through the dialogue between Maya and David, readers gain insights into how AI can assist in overcoming creative challenges and enhancing the storytelling process. The interaction highlights the benefits of integrating AI into scriptwriting, making it an engaging and informative experience for aspiring and established screenwriters alike.

Chapter 3: Generative AI in Filmmaking

3.2 Visual Storyboarding

Scene:

In a sleek, modern studio adorned with film posters and storyboards, Julia, a passionate director, is deep in the pre-production phase of her next film. She's seated at a large desk cluttered with script notes, sketches, and storyboarding materials. Enter Liam, a tech-savvy production assistant who's keen to show Julia how Generative AI can streamline the storyboarding process.

Julia: (flipping through a stack of hand-drawn storyboards) "Liam, these storyboards are coming along, but I'm feeling overwhelmed by the number of scenes we need to visualize. It's a lot of work to sketch everything out manually."

Liam: (enthusiastically) "Julia, I think I have a solution that'll make this process a lot easier. Have you ever considered using Generative AI to create storyboards?"

Julia: (curious) "Generative AI for storyboarding? I've heard about AI in filmmaking, but I didn't realize it could help with storyboarding. How does it work?"

Liam: "It's quite fascinating! AI tools can generate storyboard frames from script descriptions, allowing you to visualize scenes quickly and efficiently. You simply provide a detailed description of the scene, and the AI produces a series of storyboard frames that represent the action."

Julia: "That sounds like it could save a lot of time. How do we get started?"

Liam: (opening a laptop) "First, we'll use an AI storyboarding tool. These tools take your scene descriptions and translate them into visual frames. Let me show you how it works."

Julia: "Great, let's see how it performs."

Liam: (typing on the laptop) "We'll input a description of one of our key scenes. For example, let's describe a dramatic confrontation between the protagonist and the antagonist in a dimly lit alley."

Julia: (watching the screen) "Okay, I've entered the scene description. What's next?"

Liam: "The AI will analyze the description and generate a series of storyboard frames based on its understanding of the scene. It takes into account the setting, characters, and action to create visuals that match your description."

Julia: (seeing the storyboard frames appear) "Wow, look at these frames! The AI has captured the mood and action of the scene perfectly. It's like having a team of storyboard artists working instantly."

Liam: "Exactly. The AI can produce several variations of each frame, allowing you to choose the ones that best represent your vision. It also helps in planning shots and camera angles, making the pre-production process more efficient."

Julia: "This is impressive! Can the AI also help with different angles and shot compositions?"

Liam: "Yes, it can. You can specify different camera angles, shot types, and framing in your descriptions. The AI will incorporate these details into the storyboard frames. For example, if you want a close-up shot or a wide-angle view, you can include that in your description."

Julia: "That's fantastic. It will definitely help in visualizing the scenes from various perspectives. Can it also adjust for changes if we modify the script or scene descriptions?"

Liam: "Absolutely. The AI can quickly regenerate storyboard frames if you make changes to the script or scene descriptions. This flexibility allows you to experiment with different visual approaches and make adjustments as needed."

Julia: "How does the AI determine the visual style of the storyboards? Can we customize that?"

Liam: "Great question. Many AI storyboarding tools allow you to select or input a visual style, such as 'cinematic,' 'comic book,' or 'sketchy.' The AI then generates frames that align with the chosen style, giving you a cohesive look for your storyboards."

Julia: "That's very useful. It'll help ensure consistency in the visual presentation of our scenes. Can we also use the AI to create storyboards for complex action sequences?"

Liam: "Yes, the AI can handle complex action sequences as well. You can describe the sequence in detail, including character movements and key actions, and the AI will generate frames that depict these elements. It's particularly useful for planning intricate scenes and ensuring that all action beats are covered."

Julia: "This could really streamline our pre-production process. How do we integrate these AI-generated storyboards into our overall workflow?"

Liam: "You can integrate the AI-generated storyboards into your workflow by reviewing and selecting the frames that best represent your vision. From there, you can refine them, add annotations, and incorporate them into your production planning. The AI frames serve as a great starting point and can be used as a reference for your final storyboards."

Julia: "I'm excited to start using this. It will save us time and give us more options for visualizing our scenes."

Liam: "I'm glad you're excited! Generative AI can be a powerful tool for filmmakers, helping to visualize and plan scenes more efficiently. It's all about enhancing your creative process and allowing you to focus on the more nuanced aspects of filmmaking."

Julia: "Thank you, Liam. I'm looking forward to seeing how this tool can enhance our project."

Liam: "You're welcome, Julia. I'm sure it will be a game-changer for your film. Let's get started with integrating these storyboards into our production process."

Scene:

As Julia begins to use the AI-generated storyboards, she finds that the process of visualizing scenes becomes much more streamlined and efficient. The AI's ability to produce various visual interpretations helps her refine her vision and plan shots with greater precision. The integration of AI into the storyboarding process proves to be a valuable asset, allowing Julia to focus more on the creative aspects of filmmaking while the AI handles the initial visualization tasks.

This chapter illustrates how Generative AI can revolutionize the storyboarding process in filmmaking. By providing practical examples and showcasing the benefits of AI in visualizing scenes, it demonstrates how AI tools can enhance the efficiency and creativity of filmmakers. The interaction between Julia and Liam highlights the potential of AI to simplify complex tasks and improve the overall production workflow.

Chapter 3: Generative AI in Filmmaking

3.3 Post-Production and Editing

Scene:

In a bustling editing suite filled with multiple monitors, editing software, and piles of footage, Sarah, a dedicated film editor, is working late into the night. Her focus is on ensuring that every scene in the film flows seamlessly. Enter Max, a tech expert who has been helping Sarah integrate Generative AI into the editing process.

Sarah: (scrolling through the footage with a tired expression) "Max, I'm struggling to keep up with the color correction and ensuring that the lighting is consistent across all scenes. It's taking up so much time."

Max: (grinning) "I've got something that might lighten your workload. Have you considered using AI for post-production tasks like color correction and audio syncing?"

Sarah: (raising an eyebrow) "AI for editing? I've heard about AI in filmmaking, but I didn't realize it could be used for these tasks. How does it help?"

Max: "Generative AI can be incredibly useful in post-production. It automates tasks like color correction, audio syncing, and even adding visual effects. Let me show you how it works."

Sarah: "I'm interested. Where do we start?"

Max: (opening a software application on a monitor) "We'll start with color correction. AI tools can analyze your footage and automatically adjust the lighting and color grading to ensure consistency throughout the film."

Sarah: "That sounds promising. How does the AI know what adjustments to make?"

Max: "The AI uses machine learning algorithms to understand the color and lighting characteristics of each scene. It compares these characteristics to a reference or a set of predefined standards and then applies corrections to match the desired look."

Sarah: (watching the screen) "So, the AI can adjust for color temperature, exposure, and even white balance?"

Max: "Exactly. It can handle all those adjustments and more. For instance, if one scene is too dark or too warm compared to others, the AI can automatically correct it to ensure a cohesive visual style."

Sarah: "That would save so much time compared to manual color grading. Can it also help with audio syncing?"

Max: "Yes, it can. AI tools can synchronize audio with video by analyzing waveforms and matching them to the corresponding video frames. This means you don't have to manually adjust audio tracks to fit with the visuals."

Sarah: "That sounds like a huge time-saver. How accurate is the AI in syncing audio?"

Max: "AI has become quite accurate in this regard. It uses sophisticated algorithms to ensure that dialogue and sound effects are perfectly aligned with the action on screen. It's especially useful for handling large amounts of footage where manual syncing would be impractical."

Sarah: "That's fantastic. What about adding visual effects? Can AI assist with that as well?"

Max: "Absolutely. AI can generate and enhance visual effects by analyzing the scenes and applying effects that match the context. For example, it can create realistic smoke, fire, or magical effects based on the requirements of your film."

Sarah: "Can it handle complex effects or only simpler ones?"

Max: "AI can handle both. For complex effects, such as simulating detailed environments or intricate motion effects, the AI can use advanced algorithms to create effects that blend seamlessly with live-action footage. It's like having a virtual effects artist on your team."

Sarah: "This is incredible. How do we integrate these AI tools into our current workflow?"

Max: "You can integrate AI tools by using them in conjunction with your existing editing software. Many AI tools offer plugins or can be used as standalone applications that export results to your editing suite. You'll start by running your footage through the AI for tasks like color correction or audio syncing, and then make any final adjustments manually."

Sarah: "That sounds straightforward. Are there any limitations or things to watch out for when using AI in editing?"

Max: "One thing to keep in mind is that while AI can automate many tasks, it might not always capture the exact artistic nuances you're aiming for. It's a good idea to review the AI-generated results and make any necessary tweaks to ensure they align with your vision."

Sarah: "Got it. I'll make sure to review and refine the AI's work to match our creative goals. I'm excited to see how this can streamline our editing process."

Max: "I'm sure you'll find it immensely helpful. AI in post-production is all about enhancing your workflow and allowing you to focus more on the creative aspects of editing."

Sarah: "Thank you, Max. I'm looking forward to seeing how these tools can improve our efficiency and the final quality of the film."

Max: "You're welcome, Sarah. It's an exciting time for filmmaking, with AI offering new possibilities to enhance every aspect of the process. Let's get started and see the results for ourselves."

Scene:

As Sarah integrates AI tools into her post-production workflow, she finds that tasks like color correction, audio syncing, and adding visual effects become much more efficient. The AI's ability to handle repetitive and time-consuming tasks frees up her time to focus on the creative aspects of editing. The film benefits from a polished, cohesive look and sound, thanks to the precision and efficiency of AI.

This chapter showcases how Generative AI can revolutionize the post-production and editing phases of filmmaking. By automating complex tasks and providing advanced tools for color correction, audio syncing, and visual effects, AI helps streamline the editing process and enhances the overall quality of the film. The interaction between Sarah and Max highlights the practical benefits of AI in editing and demonstrates how these tools can integrate seamlessly into a filmmaker's workflow.

Chapter 4: Generative AI in CGI and VFX

4.1 Creating Realistic 3D Models

Scene:

In a high-tech CGI studio, the room buzzes with creative energy. Monitors display intricate 3D models of fantastical creatures and futuristic cities. Zoe, a seasoned CGI artist, is working on a new sci-fi movie. Enter Liam, a technology consultant specializing in Generative AI, who is here to help Zoe leverage AI for creating realistic 3D models.

Zoe: (studying a complex 3D model of a futuristic spaceship) "Liam, this project is ambitious. We need detailed 3D models for everything from futuristic gadgets to alien landscapes. But it's taking us a lot of time to design everything manually."

Liam: (smiling) "That's where Generative AI comes in. With AI, we can speed up the design process and create highly realistic 3D models quickly. Let me show you how."

Zoe: "I'm intrigued. How exactly can AI assist us with 3D modeling?"

Liam: "Generative AI can help by generating 3D models based on the specifications you provide. For example, if you need a model of a futuristic gadget, you can input your design parameters, and the AI will create a detailed 3D model based on those inputs."

Zoe: "That sounds promising. Can you give me an example of how this works in practice?"

Liam: "Sure. Let's say you need a detailed 3D model of an alien creature. You would start by defining some characteristics for the creature, like its size, shape, and texture. Then, you feed these parameters into an AI tool designed for 3D modeling."

Zoe: (nodding) "And the AI will generate a model based on these characteristics?"

Liam: "Exactly. The AI uses machine learning algorithms to understand the parameters and create a model that fits your description. It can also refine the details by learning from existing models and designs. This way, you get a high-quality, realistic 3D model without having to design every detail from scratch."

Zoe: "How does the AI ensure that the models it generates are realistic?"

Liam: "AI tools for 3D modeling are trained on vast datasets of existing 3D models and real-world objects. They learn from these datasets to understand what makes a model look realistic. For instance, the AI knows how to simulate textures, lighting, and shading to make the model appear lifelike."

Zoe: "Can the AI also help with designing objects that don't exist in the real world, like futuristic gadgets?"

Liam: "Yes, indeed. For objects that don't exist in reality, the AI uses creativity based on the parameters you provide. It can generate unique designs by combining elements from different models and styles, ensuring that the gadgets look futuristic and innovative."

Zoe: "How much control do we have over the final result? Can we tweak the models generated by the AI?"

Liam: "You have a lot of control. Once the AI generates a model, you can review and adjust it using standard 3D modeling software. The AI-generated model serves as a starting point or a detailed draft, which you can then refine to match your vision."

Zoe: "That's great to hear. How does this integration fit into our existing workflow?"

Liam: "You can integrate AI-generated models into your workflow by using them alongside your traditional modeling tools. Start by generating initial models with AI, and then use your expertise to enhance and finalize them. This approach allows you to focus on the creative and artistic aspects while the AI handles the more repetitive tasks."

Zoe: "It sounds like AI could really streamline our process and give us more time to focus on creativity. Are there any limitations or challenges we should be aware of?"

Liam: "One challenge is ensuring that the AI-generated models align with the artistic vision of the project. While AI can produce high-quality models, it's important to review and tweak them to ensure they meet your specific needs. Additionally, AI tools require high-quality input data and parameters to produce the best results."

Zoe: "Understood. I'm excited to see how AI can enhance our workflow. Can you show me how to use one of these AI tools?"

Liam: "Absolutely. Let's start with a demo. We'll use an AI tool to generate a 3D model based on a set of specifications. I'll guide you through the process, and you'll see firsthand how AI can assist in creating detailed and realistic models."

Scene:

As Liam demonstrates the AI tool, Zoe inputs specifications for a futuristic gadget. The AI quickly generates a detailed 3D model, complete with intricate textures and realistic lighting. Zoe is impressed by the efficiency and quality of the model.

Zoe: "This is amazing! The model looks fantastic and aligns well with our project's needs. I can't wait to integrate AI into our workflow."

Liam: "I'm glad you're excited. AI has the potential to revolutionize 3D modeling and VFX by making the design process faster and more creative. With these tools, you'll be able to bring your imaginative visions to life more efficiently."

Zoe: "Thank you, Liam. This technology is a game-changer for our industry. I'm looking forward to exploring all the possibilities it offers."

Liam: "You're welcome, Zoe. I'm excited to see what you'll create with the help of AI. Remember, the sky's the limit when it comes to creativity with these tools."

This chapter illustrates how Generative AI can transform CGI and VFX by streamlining the creation of realistic 3D models. Through a practical example, Zoe and Liam demonstrate how AI can generate detailed models based on specific parameters, enhancing both efficiency and creativity in the design process.

4.2 Enhancing Visual Effects

Scene:

In a sleek and bustling VFX studio, screens are alive with vibrant, fantastical images. Workers are focused on their screens, fine-tuning the intricate visual elements of a fantasy film. Ava, a lead VFX artist, is poring over a sequence involving a dragon's fiery breath. Ethan, an AI specialist with a knack for visual effects, enters the room with a determined look on his face.

Ava: (frustrated) "Ethan, this dragon fire effect is not blending well with the live-action footage. It looks too artificial and out of place. We need it to look more realistic."

Ethan: (enthusiastic) "I think I have just the solution. Have you ever considered using Generative AI to enhance your visual effects?"

Ava: (curious) "Generative AI for visual effects? How can that help with blending elements like fire or magical effects?"

Ethan: "Generative AI can be a game-changer for visual effects by simulating complex environmental effects such as smoke, fire, and water. Let me show you how it works."

Ava: "I'm intrigued. How does AI manage to create such realistic effects?"

Ethan: "AI uses sophisticated algorithms to simulate natural phenomena. For instance, when creating fire, the AI analyzes real-world footage of flames and combustion. It then uses this data to generate realistic fire effects that can be seamlessly integrated into your scenes."

Ava: "That sounds promising. Can you give me an example of how we might use AI to enhance our dragon fire effect?"

Ethan: "Certainly. Imagine we start by feeding the AI tool with examples of real fire footage—both natural and controlled. The AI learns from these examples to understand the patterns, colors, and movement of fire. It then applies this knowledge to generate a fire effect that looks realistic and integrates well with the live-action footage."

Ava: (nodding) "So, the AI can create a fire effect that mimics real flames in terms of appearance and behavior?"

Ethan: "Exactly. It can simulate various elements such as the flicker of flames, the way fire spreads, and even the interaction between fire and other elements like smoke. This results in visual effects that are not only realistic but also dynamically responsive to the scene."

Ava: "What about magical effects, like the glowing trails or sparkles we need for the dragon's breath?"

Ethan: "AI can handle those too. By analyzing footage of real magical effects or similar phenomena, the AI can generate intricate and realistic magical effects that match the visual style of your film. It can simulate particles, light interactions, and magical distortions with high accuracy."

Ava: "That's impressive. How does the AI ensure that these effects blend seamlessly with live-action footage?"

Ethan: "The AI uses techniques such as motion tracking and environmental mapping. It adjusts the effects to match the lighting, shadows, and movement of the live-action footage. For example, if your dragon's fire is supposed to illuminate nearby objects, the AI will ensure that the fire effect casts realistic light and shadows on those objects."

Ava: "And how do we integrate the AI-generated effects into our existing pipeline?"

Ethan: "The AI-generated effects are exported as assets that can be imported into your VFX software. From there, you can further tweak and refine them to fit your specific needs. This integration allows you to maintain control over the final look while benefiting from the AI's ability to generate high-quality effects quickly."

Ava: "What about the creative control? Can we customize the effects to fit our artistic vision?"

Ethan: "Absolutely. While the AI provides a strong starting point, you can use your artistic expertise to customize and refine the effects. You can adjust parameters like color, intensity, and behavior to ensure the effects align perfectly with your vision."

Ava: "That's great. It sounds like AI can save us a lot of time and effort while giving us high-quality results. Are there any limitations or challenges we should be aware of?"

Ethan: "One challenge is ensuring that the AI-generated effects align with the overall artistic style of the film. The AI excels at creating realistic effects, but it's important to review and adjust them to ensure they fit seamlessly into your unique visual style. Additionally, high-quality input data is crucial for the AI to generate accurate and effective results."

Ava: "Understood. I'm excited to see how AI can enhance our visual effects. Can you show me a demo of the AI in action?"

Ethan: "Certainly. Let's start by feeding the AI tool with some sample footage of fire and magical effects. We'll then generate a new effect and integrate it into a test scene to see how it performs."

Scene:

Ethan and Ava work together to input sample footage into the AI tool. The AI quickly generates a stunning fire effect and magical trails that blend seamlessly with the live-action dragon footage. Ava is impressed by the realistic and dynamic results.

Ava: "This is fantastic! The fire looks incredibly realistic, and the magical trails are perfect. I can see how AI will make a huge difference in our workflow."

Ethan: "I'm glad you think so. AI has the potential to revolutionize visual effects by providing powerful tools for creating realistic and dynamic effects quickly. With these tools, you can push the boundaries of what's possible in filmmaking."

Ava: "Thank you, Ethan. This technology will definitely enhance our creative possibilities and streamline our process. I'm looking forward to exploring it further."

Ethan: "You're welcome, Ava. I'm excited to see how you'll use AI to bring your creative vision to life. Remember, the possibilities are as vast as your imagination."

This chapter demonstrates how Generative AI can enhance visual effects by simulating realistic environmental effects like fire, smoke, and magical elements.

Through a practical example, Ava and Ethan showcase how AI-generated effects can seamlessly integrate with live-action footage, providing high-quality results and creative flexibility.

4.3 Automating Animation

Scene:

In a state-of-the-art animation studio, the walls are adorned with concept art and character designs. The air is filled with the hum of computers and the chatter of animators discussing their latest projects. At a central workstation, Jamie, an experienced animator, is facing a dilemma: the animation project is behind schedule, and the task of creating in-between frames is proving to be time-consuming. Riley, an AI specialist with a keen interest in animation, walks over with a confident stride.

Jamie: (frustrated) "Riley, I'm drowning in in-between frames for this character animation. It's taking forever, and we're falling behind on the schedule. Is there any way to speed this up?"

Riley: (smiling) "Actually, there is! Have you ever considered using AI to automate some of the animation processes? It can make a huge difference."

Jamie: (curious) "AI for animation? I've heard about it but never really looked into how it works. How can AI help with creating in-between frames?"

Riley: "AI can be incredibly helpful for automating the creation of in-between frames, a process known as 'inbetweening' or 'tweening.' By using AI tools, you can significantly reduce the time and effort needed to create smooth transitions between keyframes."

Jamie: "That sounds interesting. But how does AI manage to generate in-between frames? Doesn't it need to understand the movement and context?"

Riley: "Yes, exactly! AI tools designed for animation work by analyzing the keyframes you provide. These keyframes represent the start and end points of a movement. The AI then uses this information to generate the intermediate frames that fill in the gaps, creating a smooth animation."

Jamie: "So, if I provide the AI with two keyframes of a character moving from one pose to another, it can create the frames in between?"

Riley: "Exactly. The AI uses algorithms that analyze the motion and interpolate the in-between frames. It understands the movement pattern, such as how the character's limbs should move and how their body should shift. The result is a smooth animation that seamlessly transitions between the keyframes."

Jamie: "That sounds like it could save us a lot of time. But how accurate is the AI in generating these frames? Will it match the style and fluidity of the animation?"

Riley: "AI tools are designed to be highly accurate and can produce frames that match the style and fluidity of the animation. Some advanced AI systems can even learn from your existing animation style and adapt their output accordingly. However, it's always a good idea to review the AI-generated frames and make any necessary adjustments to ensure they align perfectly with your vision."

Jamie: "What about creating realistic movements based on motion capture data? Can AI help with that as well?"

Riley: "Absolutely. AI can enhance motion capture data by analyzing the captured movements and generating realistic animations. For instance, if you have motion capture data of a character running, the AI can use this data to create a more fluid and natural animation by smoothing out any inconsistencies and adding realistic motion details."

Jamie: "That's impressive. How do we integrate AI-generated animations into our existing workflow?"

Riley: "AI-generated frames can be exported as assets and imported into your animation software. From there, you can further refine and adjust them to fit your project's needs. The AI acts as a powerful tool to streamline your workflow, allowing you to focus on more creative aspects of the animation."

Jamie: "Can you show me how this works in practice? I'd love to see a demo of AI generating in-between frames."

Riley: "Sure thing. Let's start by loading some keyframes into the AI tool. We'll generate the in-between frames and see how well it integrates with the existing animation. I'll also show you how to review and adjust the results."

Scene:

Riley and Jamie begin by uploading keyframes of a character's movement into the AI tool. The AI quickly generates a series of in-between frames, creating a smooth and fluid animation sequence. Jamie is amazed by the results, noting how well the AI's output matches the desired style and movement.

Jamie: "This is fantastic! The AI-generated frames look incredibly smooth and fit perfectly with the animation. This will definitely help us meet our deadlines."

Riley: "I'm glad you like it. AI has the potential to transform animation by automating repetitive tasks and enhancing the quality of the final product. With these tools, you can push the boundaries of creativity while saving time and effort."

Jamie: "Thank you, Riley. I'm excited to incorporate AI into our workflow. It feels like a whole new world of possibilities has opened up."

Riley: "You're welcome, Jamie. Remember, AI is a powerful collaborator that can help you achieve new levels of creativity and efficiency. The more you explore and integrate these tools, the more you'll discover their potential."

Scene:

As Riley and Jamie continue working together, the studio buzzes with renewed energy. The integration of AI into their animation process has not only improved efficiency but also opened up new avenues for creative exploration. The potential of AI to enhance animation and VFX is now a reality, transforming the way they approach their craft.

This chapter highlights how Generative AI can automate aspects of animation, such as creating in-between frames and enhancing movements based on motion capture data. Through a practical demonstration, Jamie and Riley showcase the benefits of AI in streamlining animation workflows, improving efficiency, and enabling creative possibilities.

Chapter 5: Getting Started with Generative AI

5.1 Choosing the Right Tools

Scene:

In a vibrant art studio, filled with canvases, digital tablets, and creative clutter, Mia, an aspiring artist, is surrounded by various AI tools and resources. She's on a mission to find the perfect AI tool to enhance her creative process. Enter Sam, an experienced digital artist and AI enthusiast, who's here to guide Mia through the selection process.

Mia: (frustratedly browsing through a list of tools) "Sam, I'm overwhelmed by all these AI tools available. How do I know which one is right for my work?"

Sam: (smiling reassuringly) "Don't worry, Mia. Finding the right AI tool is all about understanding your needs and matching them with the capabilities of the tool. Let's break it down."

Mia: (curious) "Okay, where should we start?"

Sam: "Let's start with art. For creating images from text prompts, tools like DALL-E and Midjourney are excellent choices. They allow you to generate visuals based on descriptive text, making them perfect for artists who want to experiment with different ideas quickly."

Mia: (interested) "How do these tools actually work?"

Sam: "DALL-E and Midjourney use advanced neural networks to understand and interpret your text prompts. For example, if you describe a 'magical forest with glowing creatures,' these tools can generate a stunning, imaginative image based on your description. It's like having a digital painter who brings your words to life."

Mia: "That sounds amazing! What about tools for filmmaking?"

Sam: "For filmmaking, you might want to explore tools like ScriptAI and DeepArt. ScriptAI helps with scriptwriting by suggesting plot twists, dialogue, and character development. It's like having a brainstorming partner who's always ready with fresh ideas."

Mia: "And DeepArt?"

Sam: "DeepArt is fantastic for visual effects. It can transform raw footage into visually stunning scenes by applying artistic styles or enhancing visual elements.

It's like having a digital effects artist who can take your footage and make it look like a masterpiece."

Mia: "Great! What about CGI and VFX?"

Sam: "For CGI and VFX, Blender with AI plugins is a top choice. Blender is a powerful 3D modeling tool, and with AI plugins, it can automate tasks like texture generation, object modeling, and even animation. It's like having a versatile toolkit that gets smarter with each update."

Mia: (nodding) "Got it. So, it's all about matching the tool to the specific needs of my project."

Sam: "Exactly. Each tool has its unique strengths, so understanding what you need will help you select the right one."

5.2 Learning and Integration

Scene:

In Mia's studio, the walls are now adorned with sketches and digital prints from various AI tools. Mia is eager to dive into learning how to use these tools effectively. Sam is here to help her start experimenting and integrating AI into her creative process.

Mia: (enthusiastically) "Sam, I'm ready to start experimenting with these tools. How should I go about it?"

Sam: "That's the spirit! The best way to get started is by experimenting with free or trial versions of the tools. Most of them come with tutorials and guides to help you learn the basics."

Mia: "That sounds manageable. What's the first step?"

Sam: "Let's begin with a simple project to get a feel for the tools. How about using an AI tool to generate a piece of art or create a storyboard for a short film? We'll follow a step-by-step tutorial together."

Mia: "Sounds perfect. Which tool should we start with?"

Sam: "Let's use DALL-E for creating a piece of art. It's user-friendly and will give you a quick sense of how AI can transform your ideas into visuals."

Scene:

Mia and Sam sit at a computer, and Sam guides Mia through the process of using DALL-E. They start by entering a text prompt—"a tranquil lake surrounded by towering mountains at sunset." The tool generates several variations of the image based on the description.

Mia: (excitedly) "Wow, these images are incredible! Each one has a unique interpretation of my description."

Sam: "Exactly. Now, take some time to explore different prompts and see how the tool responds. Document your process and reflect on the results. This will help you understand the tool's capabilities and limitations."

Mia: "I'll definitely do that. What should I keep in mind while experimenting?"

Sam: "Pay attention to how well the AI captures the essence of your prompts. Notice the details, colors, and overall composition. Also, think about how you can incorporate these AI-generated pieces into your larger creative project."

Mia: "Got it. I'm excited to see what else I can create!"

Sam: "Fantastic! As you continue experimenting, you'll start to discover new ways to use AI in your work. Remember, the key is to explore, reflect, and integrate what you learn into your creative process."

5.3 Ethical Considerations

Scene:

In a cozy corner of Mia's studio, she and Sam sit surrounded by various AI-generated artworks and footage. Mia is deep in thought about the ethical implications of using AI in her creative work. Sam is ready to provide guidance on this important topic.

Mia: (thoughtfully) "Sam, I've been thinking about the ethical aspects of using AI. How can I ensure that my AI-generated content is used responsibly?"

Sam: "That's an important consideration, Mia. There are several key ethical aspects to keep in mind when working with AI."

Mia: "Such as?"

Sam: "First, ensure that the AI-generated content is original and doesn't infringe on the rights of other creators. Even though AI tools generate new content, they're trained on existing data, so it's crucial to verify that your work doesn't unintentionally replicate someone else's intellectual property."

Mia: "How can I check for originality?"

Sam: "You can use tools to check for plagiarism or duplicate content. Additionally, familiarize yourself with the terms of service of the AI tools you're using, as they often include guidelines on copyright and usage."

Mia: "What about the ethical use of AI-generated content?"

Sam: "Be transparent about your use of AI in your work. If you're using AI tools to create art or generate content, acknowledge this in your presentations or publications. It's also important to respect the privacy and data rights of individuals if your AI tools involve personal or sensitive information."

Mia: "I'll definitely keep that in mind. Is there anything else I should be aware of?"

Sam: "Consider the broader impact of your AI-generated work. Think about how it might influence your audience and how it aligns with your values. Using AI responsibly involves being mindful of both the creative and ethical dimensions of your work."

Mia: "Thanks for the guidance, Sam. I feel more confident about navigating these ethical considerations."

Sam: "You're welcome, Mia. Ethical considerations are a vital part of the creative process. By being mindful and responsible, you can ensure that your use of AI contributes positively to your art and to the broader creative community."

Scene:

As Mia and Sam continue their discussion, the studio's atmosphere becomes one of thoughtful reflection. Mia is now equipped not only with the tools to enhance her creativity but also with a clear understanding of the ethical responsibilities that come with using AI in her work. The integration of AI into her artistic process is now guided by both technical skill and ethical awareness.

This chapter provides a comprehensive guide for getting started with Generative AI, from choosing the right tools and learning how to use them, to navigating ethical considerations. By incorporating practical examples, interactive elements, and a focus on responsible use, it ensures that readers can confidently explore and integrate AI into their creative endeavors.

Chapter 6:
Case Studies and
Success Stories

6.1 Artistic Triumphs

Scene:

In a bustling art gallery, visitors admire a series of stunning digital paintings displayed in well-lit frames. Emma, now a renowned digital artist, walks through the gallery with her mentor, Sam. They pause in front of a particularly striking piece.

Emma: (proudly) "Sam, this is where it all began. I used AI to create these paintings. Each piece is inspired by different prompts I fed into the AI tool."

Sam: (admiring the artwork) "It's incredible, Emma. How did you first get the idea to use AI in your art?"

Emma: "I was initially skeptical, but once I started experimenting with DALL-E and Midjourney, I realized how AI could help me explore new artistic directions. For instance, I wanted to create a series of abstract landscapes that combined elements of surrealism and impressionism. Using AI, I could generate multiple variations of these concepts quickly, which helped me find a unique style."

Sam: "It's fascinating to see how you've blended traditional artistic sensibilities with modern technology. Can you share how the integration of AI influenced the final results?"

Emma: "Absolutely. The AI helped me visualize concepts that were beyond my initial imagination. By generating numerous drafts and iterations, I could refine my ideas and focus on the elements that resonated with me. For example, one of the pieces here was inspired by a dream I described to the AI. The result was something I wouldn't have thought of on my own, but it perfectly captured the mood I was aiming for."

Sam: "And how was the reception to your work?"

Emma: "The gallery's response has been overwhelmingly positive. People are intrigued by the fusion of AI and traditional art. They appreciate the innovative approach and the way AI has expanded the possibilities of artistic expression."

Sam: "Your success is a testament to how AI can enhance creativity and open new avenues for artists. It's clear that AI isn't just a tool but a collaborator in your artistic journey."

Emma: "Exactly. It's about finding the balance between human creativity and technological innovation."

6.2 Filmmaking Innovations

Scene:

In a cutting-edge film studio, the buzz of excitement is palpable as the crew gathers around a computer screen showcasing a breathtaking visual effect. Mia, now an accomplished filmmaker, discusses her latest project with her colleagues.

Mia: "Everyone, check out this scene from our latest film. We used AI to create some of the most complex visual effects we've ever done."

Colleague 1: "Wow, the level of detail is incredible. How did AI play a role in this?"

Mia: "We used an AI tool for generating visual effects that involved simulating realistic environmental elements like fire and water. For example, in one scene, a dragon breathes fire during an intense battle. The AI helped us create realistic flames that interacted dynamically with the environment."

Colleague 2: "That must have saved a lot of time compared to traditional methods."

Mia: "Absolutely. AI allowed us to experiment with different fire and smoke simulations quickly, which meant we could focus on perfecting the shot rather than getting bogged down with the technical details. Plus, it gave us creative freedom to explore effects that would have been challenging to achieve manually."

Colleague 3: "And what was the audience's reaction?"

Mia: "The feedback has been fantastic. Audiences are raving about the film's visual spectacle. The AI-generated effects have added a new layer of immersion and realism that has really resonated with viewers."

Colleague 1: "It sounds like AI has significantly enhanced your filmmaking process."

Mia: "It definitely has. AI has streamlined our workflows and allowed us to push the boundaries of what's possible in visual storytelling. It's a game-changer in the industry."

6.3 CGI and VFX Milestones

Scene:

In a bustling VFX studio, artists and technicians work diligently on computers, surrounded by screens displaying intricate animations. Alex, the head of the VFX team, proudly shows off their latest project—a major video game with stunning visual effects.

Alex: "Everyone, gather around. I want to show you how AI has played a pivotal role in our latest game's animations."

Team Member: "What's the breakthrough this time?"

Alex: "We used AI to generate complex animations for the game's character movements and environments. For instance, we needed a realistic simulation of a character's fluid movements during combat scenes. AI helped us automate the creation of in-between frames, ensuring smooth and lifelike animation."

Team Member: "That sounds impressive. How did AI improve the animation process?"

Alex: "Traditionally, animating complex sequences like these required a lot of manual work. With AI, we could input a few keyframes, and the system generated the in-between frames, saving us countless hours of manual animation. It also helped in generating textures and environmental details that would have been time-consuming to create from scratch."

Team Member: "What about the results?"

Alex: "The feedback from players has been phenomenal. The animations are fluid and immersive, enhancing the overall gameplay experience. AI has allowed us to achieve a level of detail and realism that sets this game apart from others."

Team Member: "It's amazing to see how AI can transform the gaming industry."

Alex: "Indeed. AI is not just a tool but a critical component of our creative process. It has expanded our capabilities and allowed us to innovate in ways we couldn't have imagined before."

Scene:

As the chapter concludes, the impact of Generative AI across various creative fields is evident. From artistic triumphs and filmmaking innovations to groundbreaking advancements in CGI and VFX, AI has proven to be a powerful catalyst for creativity and efficiency. The stories shared highlight the transformative potential of AI, showcasing its ability to enhance artistic expression, streamline production processes, and achieve high-quality results in the world of digital art and entertainment.

This chapter emphasizes that AI is not just a tool but a collaborator that, when used effectively, can elevate creative projects and open new horizons for artists, filmmakers, and VFX professionals alike

Chapter 7: Future Trends and Innovations

7.1 The Evolution of Generative AI

Scene:

In a futuristic laboratory filled with holographic displays and cutting-edge technology, Dr. Ava Chen, a leading AI researcher, and Jordan, a passionate creative technologist, are discussing the future of Generative AI. The room is bathed in soft blue light, giving it an ethereal, forward-looking atmosphere.

Jordan: (gesturing to a holographic projection of an AI model) "Ava, it's incredible to see how far generative AI has come. What do you think the future holds for this technology?"

Ava: (nodding thoughtfully) "The evolution of generative AI is going to be both fascinating and transformative. We're already seeing significant advancements in how AI can generate content, but the future promises even more revolutionary changes."

Jordan: "Such as?"

Ava: "For starters, we're likely to see AI models that are more adaptive and context-aware. Imagine an AI that not only creates art or film but understands and adapts to the evolving preferences and emotional states of its users. It could generate content that feels more personalized and resonant."

Jordan: "That sounds almost like AI could develop a sense of emotional intelligence."

Ava: "In a way, yes. While AI won't experience emotions, future models will be better at interpreting and responding to human emotions and context. This means more nuanced and engaging creative works. For example, AI could tailor a film's narrative or an artwork's theme based on audience feedback in real-time."

Jordan: "What about the technical aspects? Are there any breakthroughs on the horizon?"

Ava: "Absolutely. We're developing new algorithms that improve the efficiency and creativity of AI models. For instance, advancements in neural architecture will enable AI to handle more complex tasks with greater precision. We'll also see improvements in multimodal AI, where a single model can integrate and generate content across different mediums—like combining text, images, and sound seamlessly."

Jordan: "How will these advancements impact the art world and entertainment industries?"

Ava: "The implications are enormous. In art, AI could enable completely new forms of creative expression, blending styles and genres in ways we've never seen. In filmmaking, AI might automate more complex aspects of production, such as dynamic storytelling or interactive experiences. For VFX, it could mean even more realistic simulations and faster turnaround times."

Jordan: "And what about the ethical and societal impacts?"

Ava: "That's a crucial consideration. As AI becomes more integrated into creative processes, we'll need to address issues of authorship, copyright, and the potential for misuse. It's important to ensure that AI tools are used responsibly and that they enhance human creativity without replacing it."

Jordan: "So, the future of generative AI is not just about technological innovation but also about navigating new ethical landscapes."

Ava: "Exactly. It's a balance of pushing the boundaries of what's possible while remaining mindful of the implications for creators and society."

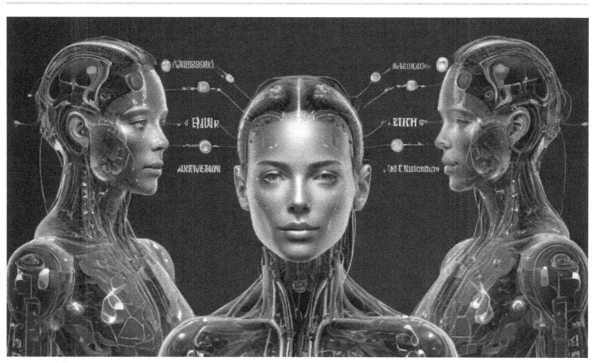

7.2 Embracing the Future

Scene:

Back in the cozy attic room, Emma, now a seasoned artist and AI enthusiast, is hosting a workshop for aspiring creatives eager to dive into the world of generative AI. The room is filled with eager participants, each with a laptop or tablet ready to explore the possibilities.

Emma: (addressing the group) "Welcome, everyone! I'm thrilled to have you here as we explore the exciting world of generative AI. Today, we'll be diving into some of the latest tools and trends in AI to see how they can enhance your creative projects."

Participant 1: "What's the first step in getting started with these new AI tools?"

Emma: "Great question. The first step is to familiarize yourself with the tools and understand their capabilities. Many AI platforms offer tutorials and demo versions that you can experiment with. I recommend starting with something simple, like generating a piece of art or a short story."

Participant 2: "Can you give us an example of a project we might work on?"

Emma: "Certainly! Let's do a fun interactive project. We'll use an AI tool to create a unique piece of digital art based on a prompt you choose. For instance, you could describe a fantastical scene or an abstract concept, and the AI will generate a series of images based on your description."

Participant 3: "How can we share and reflect on our results?"

Emma: "Once you've generated your artworks, we'll set up a shared online gallery where everyone can upload their creations. You can write a brief reflection on how the AI influenced your work and what you learned from the process. It's a great way to see different approaches and get feedback from others."

Participant 4: "What should we keep in mind while using these tools?"

Emma: "As you experiment with AI, remember to think about the ethical implications and how you're integrating AI into your creative practice. Ensure that your use of AI respects intellectual property rights and contributes positively to your artistic vision."

Participant 1: "I'm excited to get started. This seems like an amazing opportunity to explore new creative possibilities."

Emma: "I'm glad you're excited! Embracing generative AI is about more than just using new technology—it's about pushing the boundaries of your creativity and discovering how AI can be a valuable collaborator in your artistic journey."

Interactive Example:

Project Brief:

Create a unique piece of digital art using an AI tool. Choose a prompt or description that inspires you, and let the AI generate multiple variations. Reflect on how the AI's interpretation aligns with your vision and what new insights or ideas emerged from the process.

Steps:

1. Choose Your Tool: Select an AI tool like DALL-E, Midjourney, or any other creative AI platform that generates visual content.

2. Craft Your Prompt: Write a descriptive prompt for the AI, such as "a magical forest at dusk" or "a futuristic city skyline."

3. Generate Art: Use the AI tool to generate several variations of your chosen prompt. Experiment with different styles and settings if the tool allows.

4. Upload and Share: Upload your creations to the shared online gallery set up for this workshop.

5. Reflect: Write a brief reflection on your experience, addressing how the AI's output differed from your expectations and what new ideas or techniques you discovered.

Encouragement:

Stay curious and open-minded as you explore these new tools. The future of AI in creativity is incredibly promising, and your experiments today could pave the way for exciting new developments in your artistic practice.

Conclusion:

Generative AI is poised to continue its transformative impact on the creative world. As technology advances, artists, filmmakers, and VFX professionals will have even more powerful tools at their disposal. By staying informed about the latest trends and innovations, and by embracing the creative potential of AI, you can push the boundaries of your work and explore new artistic horizons.

Remember, the journey with AI is not just about adopting new tools but about continually experimenting, reflecting, and adapting. The possibilities are vast, and your imagination is the only limit. Embrace the future of generative AI and let it inspire your next creative masterpiece.

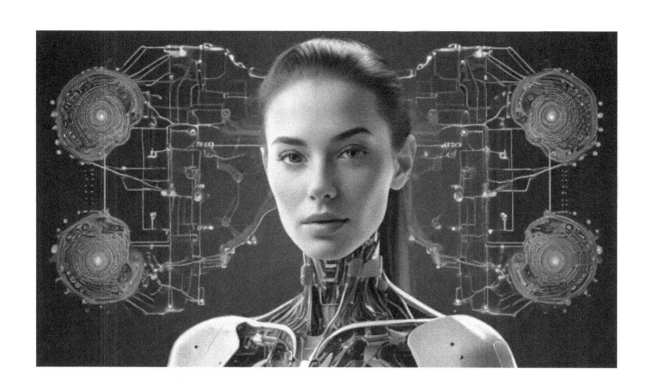

Conclusion

Generative AI is reshaping the creative landscape in profound and exciting ways. As we navigate through this transformative era, it becomes evident that AI is not merely a tool but a powerful ally in the realm of art, filmmaking, and visual effects. Its ability to generate innovative content, enhance creative processes, and offer fresh perspectives is unlocking unprecedented opportunities for artists, filmmakers, and VFX professionals alike.

A New Era of Creativity

Generative AI empowers creators to transcend traditional boundaries and explore new dimensions of artistic expression. For artists, AI provides a collaborative partner capable of producing novel designs and experimenting with styles that might have been previously unimaginable. Filmmakers can leverage AI to streamline scriptwriting, visualize scenes with advanced storyboarding, and refine post-production with precision. In the world of CGI and VFX, AI enhances the realism of 3D models, visual effects, and animation, transforming the way we bring imaginative worlds to life.

Enhancing Artistic Processes

The integration of AI into creative workflows offers numerous advantages:

- Creativity Amplified: AI tools can suggest new ideas, generate drafts, and explore styles, allowing artists to push the boundaries of their work and discover new forms of expression.

- Efficiency Unleashed: By automating repetitive tasks and streamlining processes, AI frees up valuable time for creatives to focus on more intricate and imaginative aspects of their projects.

- Personalized Innovation: As AI evolves, it will increasingly adapt to individual preferences and contexts, offering more personalized and resonant creative solutions.

Navigating the Future

Looking ahead, the future of generative AI holds exciting possibilities:

- Advanced AI Models: Expect more sophisticated AI systems that understand and respond to complex creative needs, providing even more nuanced and contextually relevant outputs.

- Ethical Considerations: As AI becomes more integrated into creative processes, it's crucial to address ethical concerns such as copyright, authorship, and the responsible use of AI-generated content.

- Continual Exploration: The field of generative AI is rapidly evolving. Staying informed about the latest developments and continually experimenting with new tools will be key to harnessing AI's full potential.

Encouraging Exploration

As you embark on your journey with generative AI, embrace the opportunities it presents. Experiment with different tools, explore new creative techniques, and reflect on how AI can enhance and expand your artistic practice. The journey with AI is not just about adopting new technology but about discovering new ways to express your creativity and pushing the boundaries of what's possible.

Generative AI is a gateway to a future where creativity knows no bounds. By understanding and leveraging these technologies, you can enhance your work, streamline your processes, and unlock new realms of artistic expression. Embrace the possibilities, stay curious, and let generative AI inspire your next creative masterpiece.

Thank you for joining us on this exploration of generative AI. May your creative endeavors be enriched and your artistic vision expanded by the boundless possibilities that AI offers.